Pebble® Plus

Monkeys

Tamarin Monkeys

by Mary R. Dunn

Consulting Editor: Gail Saunders-Smith, PhD

Consultant: Lori Perkins,
Vice President of Collections
Zoo Atlanta, Atlanta, Georgia

CAPSTONE PRESS
a capstone imprint

Pebble Plus is published by Capstone Press,
1710 Roe Crest Drive, North Mankato, Minnesota 56003.
www.capstonepub.com

Library of Congress Cataloging-in-Publication Data
Dunn, Mary R.
Tamarin monkeys / by Mary Dunn.
p. cm.—(Pebble Plus. Monkeys)
Includes bibliographical references and index.
Summary: "Full-color photographs and simple text introduce tamarin monkeys"—Provided by publisher.
ISBN 978-1-62065-105-6 (library binding)
ISBN 978-1-4765-1083-5 (eBook PDF)
1. Tamarins—Juvenile literature. I. Title.
QL737.P925D86 2013
599.8′4—dc23   2012023415

Editorial Credits
Jeni Wittrock, editor; Bobbie Nuytten, designer; Svetlana Zhurkin, media researcher; Eric Manske, production specialist

Photo Credits
Alamy: Arco Images GmbH, 7, Linda Kennedy, 17, Niels Poulsen, 11, Sean O'Neill, 15; Minden Pictures: SA Team, 13; Nature Picture Library: Lisa Hoffner, 9; Shutterstock: DJP3tros, 21, Dr. Morley Read, 19, Eric Gevaert, cover, 1, 5

Note to Parents and Teachers

The Monkeys set supports national science standards related to life science. This book describes and illustrates tamarin monkeys. The images support early readers in understanding the text. The repetition of words and phrases helps early readers learn new words. This book also introduces early readers to subject-specific vocabulary words, which are defined in the Glossary section. Early readers may need assistance to read some words and to use the Table of Contents, Glossary, Read More, Internet Sites, and Index sections of the book.

Printed in the United States of America in North Mankato, Minnesota.
092012   006933CGS13

Table of Contents

Wild and Woolly

Tamarins are small monkeys

with showy, colorful hair.

Some tamarins have

fluffy white mohawks.

Others have mustaches!

There are more than 40 kinds of tamarins. They all live in Central and South America. Around nine tamarins live together in a family group.

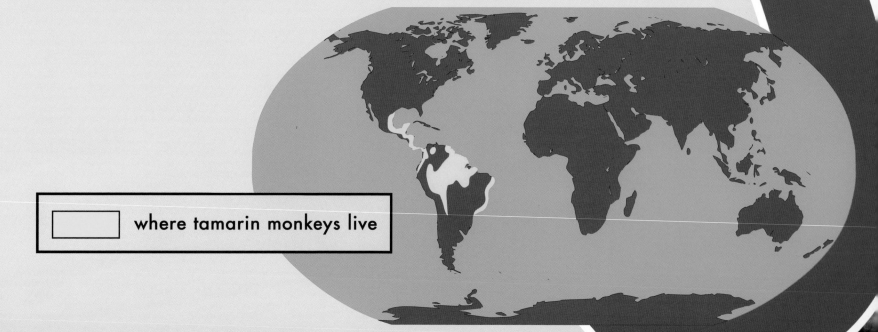

where tamarin monkeys live

Tree Monkeys

Tamarin families live high in the trees. They leap from vines and branches in their leafy homes. At night, these mammals rest in tree holes.

Tamarins' bodies are perfect for forest living. They use their long tails to balance. Their clawlike nails scratch for insects and sap to eat.

golden lion tamarin
10 inches
(25 centimeters)

6 feet
(183 cm)

Finding Food

Tamarins usually search
for fruit in early morning.
Some snack on lizards and
frogs too. Tamarins share their
food with their family group.

13

Growing Up

Female tamarins have
one or two litters of twins
each year. Baby tamarins
are covered in hair. They drink
their mother's milk.

Father tamarins help care for the newborns. Older relatives babysit the young twins. In the wild, tamarins live about 12 years.

In Danger

Many tamarins are in danger
of losing their forest homes.
People cut down trees
to make room for houses,
farms, and roads.

Groups of tamarins stick together to avoid predators. Tamarins keep watch for snakes, eagles, and jaguars.

Glossary

balance—to keep steady and not fall over

insect—a small animal with a hard outer shell, six legs, three body sections, and two antennae; most insects have wings

litter—a group of animals born at the same time to the same mother

mammal—a warm-blooded animal that breathes air; a mammal has hair or fur; female mammals feed milk to their young

mohawk—a hairstyle with very short hair except for a center strip of long hair

mustache—hair that grows on a monkey's top lip

nail—a hard covering on the finger or toe of a monkey

predator—an animal that hunts other animals for food

showy—flashy and bold

vine—a plant with a long, thin stem that climbs trees

Read More

Bodden, Valerie. *Monkeys*. Amazing Animals. Mankato, Minn.: Creative Education, 2010.

Gosman, Gillian. *Tamarins*. Monkey Business. New York: PowerKids Press, 2012.

Somervill, Barbara A. *Road to Recovery: Golden Lion Tamarin*. 21st Century Skills Library. Ann Arbor, Mich.: Cherry Lake Pub., 2008.

Internet Sites

FactHound offers a safe, fun way to find Internet sites related to this book. All of the sites on FactHound have been researched by our staff.

Here's all you do:

Visit *www.facthound.com*

Type in this code: 9781620651056

Super-cool stuff! Check out projects, games and lots more at www.capstonekids.com

Index

Word Count: 195
Grade: 1
Early-Intervention Level: 21